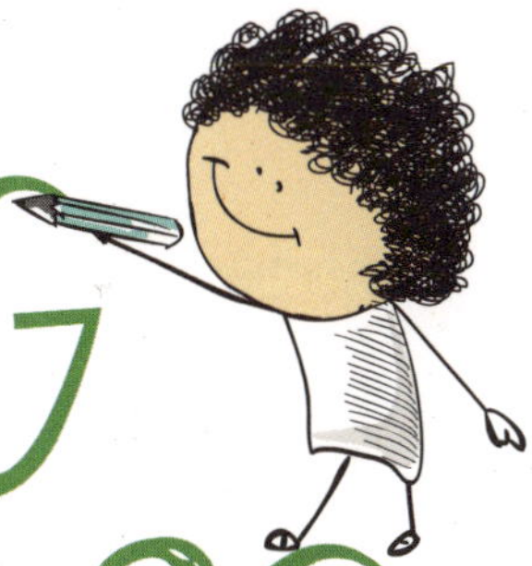

DRAWING & PAINTING TECHNIQUES

WORKBOOK

Level 2

Om KIDZ

An imprint of Om Books International

Border Beauty

Practice the borders. Then, stick a family photograph in the space given below and draw a beautiful border around it.

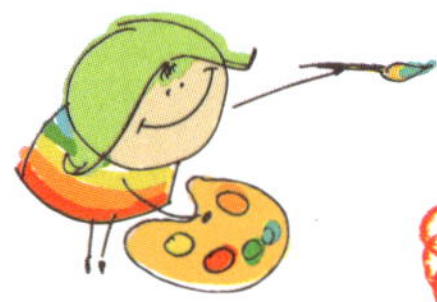

Make your painting a masterpiece by adding a border to it.

Paste your family picture here.

Chicken Fingers

Dip your finger in paint and make a "J". When the paint dries, make eyes and feet for the chickens. You can also flip the "J". Use as many colours as you can.

Paint a Pot

Follow the steps to draw this vase in the space given below.

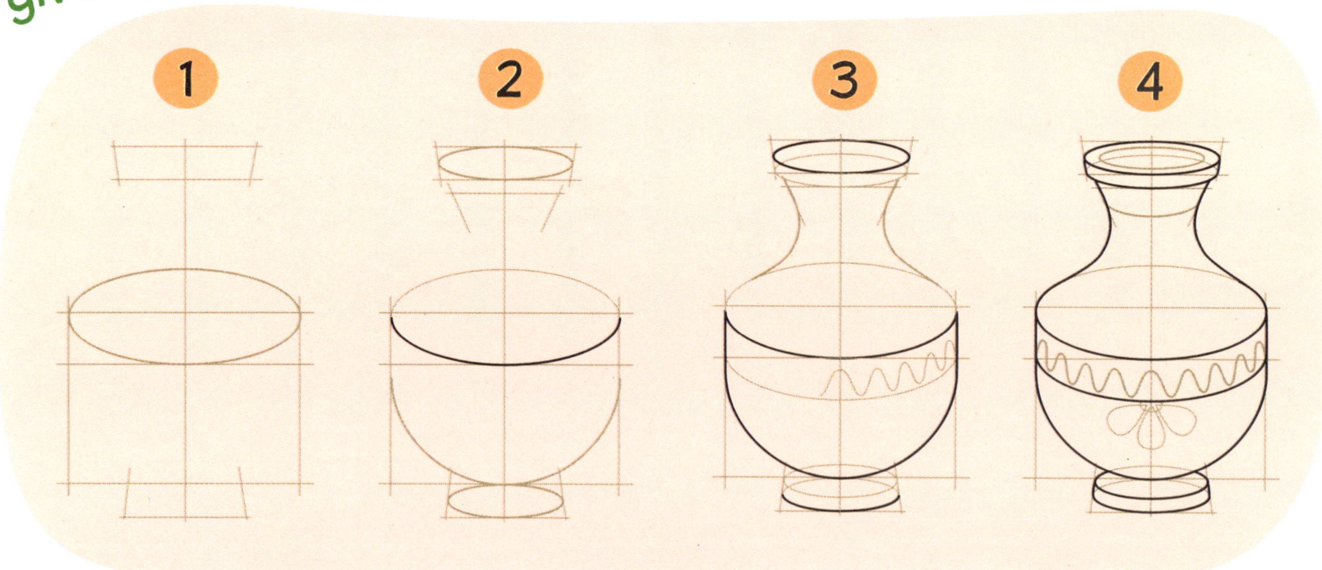

The Skylines

Draw three different skylines. Use a black sketch pen to draw different kinds of buildings.

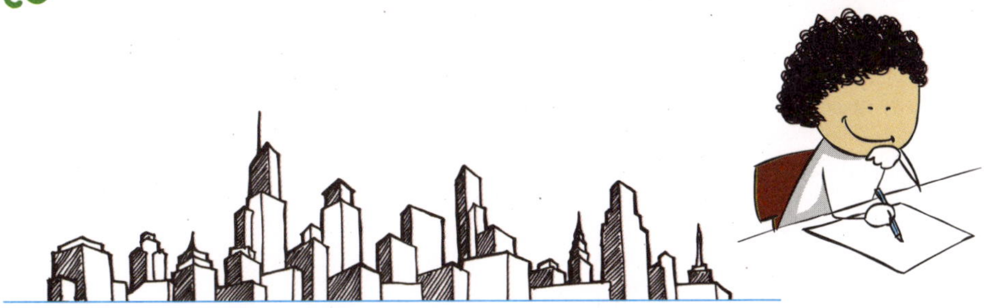

You can draw a skyline of a city, village or a landscape.

Oscar the Octopus

Use crayons to colour Oscar the octopus as shown below.

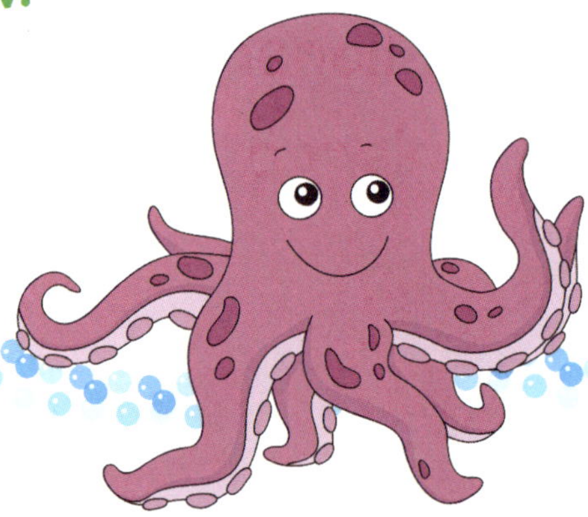

Make sure that you colour within the outline.

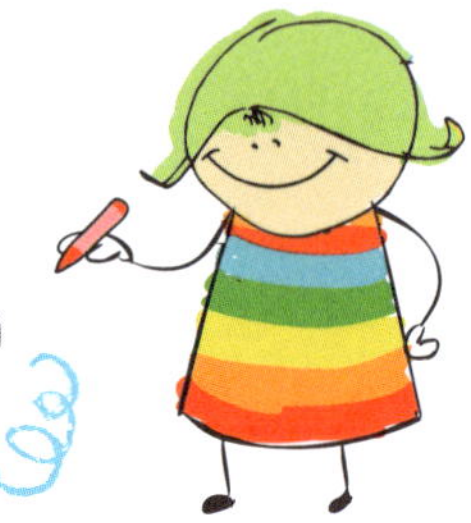

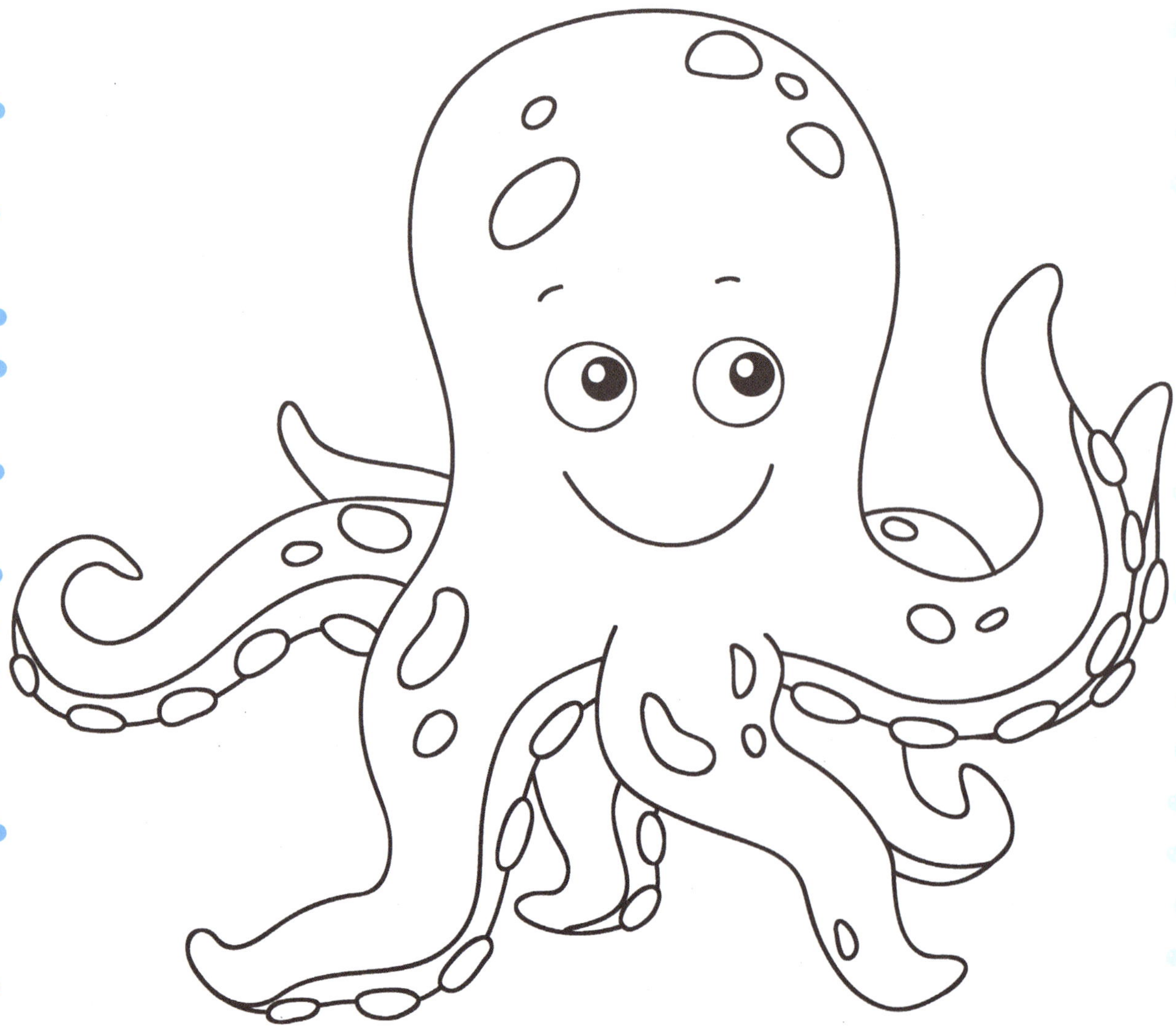

Kitty Cat

Follow these five steps given below to draw a kitten.

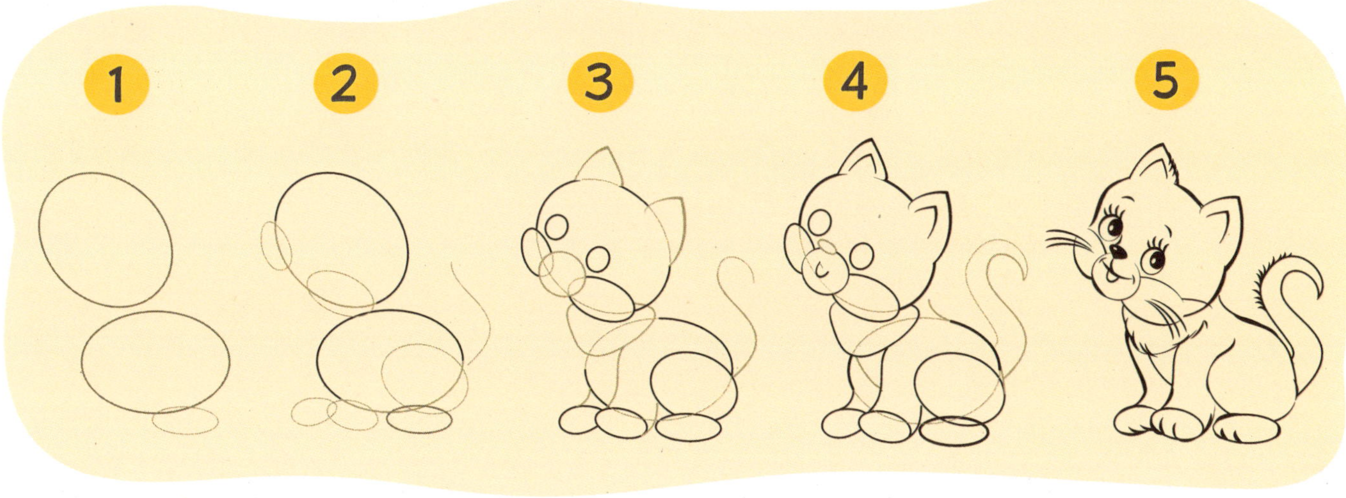

Ladyfinger Flowers

Cut a ladyfinger, dip it in thick paint and use it to make a flower bouquet below.

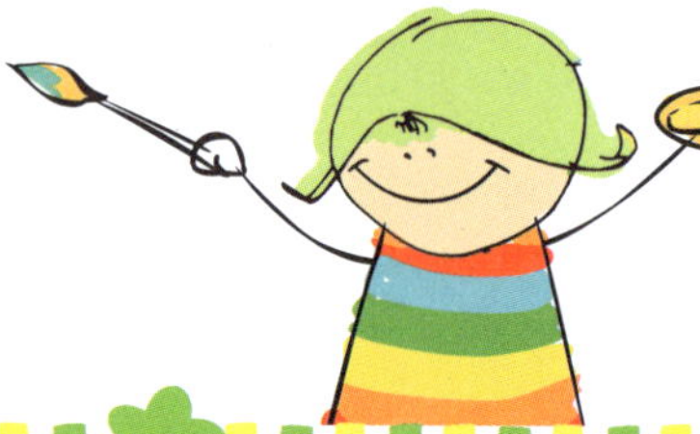

Take the help of an adult to cut the ladyfinger.

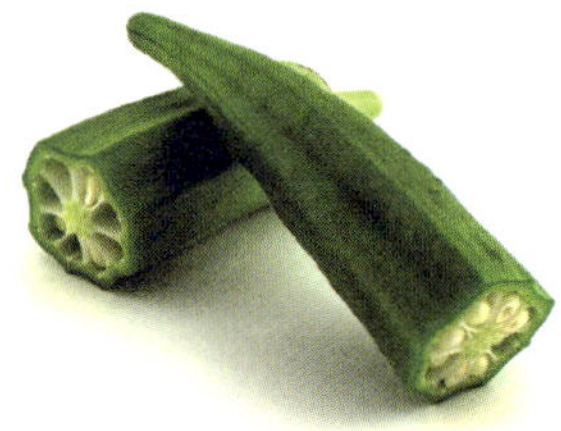

Sally the Sea Lion

Copy Sally the sea lion in the grid below. Colour the picture carefully.

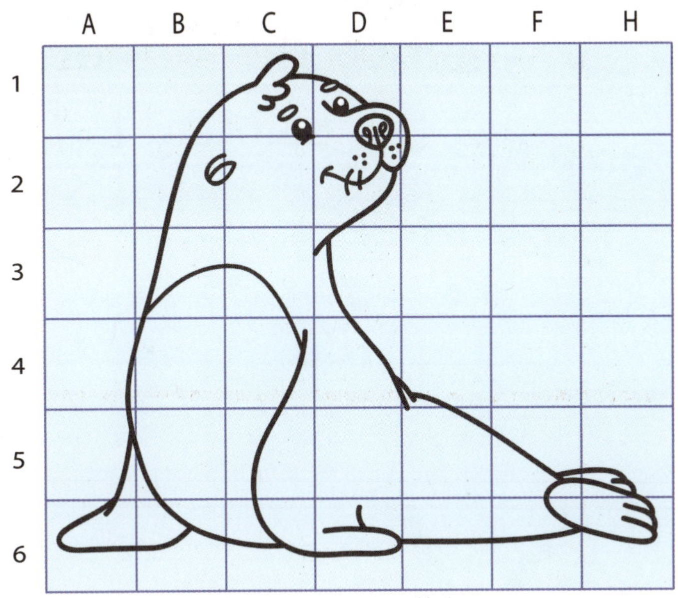

	A	B	C	D	E	F	H
1							
2							
3							
4							
5							
6							

Chinese Art

First, practice the Chinese style of painting. Then, complete the painting below using gentle strokes of black paint.

Chinese paintings are famous for their black ink. Red may be used from time to time.

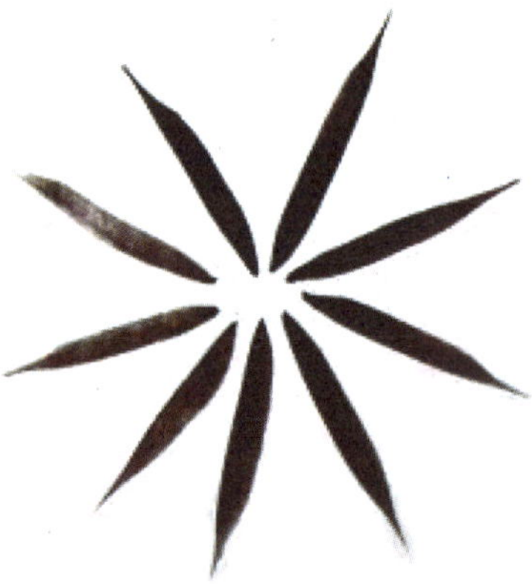

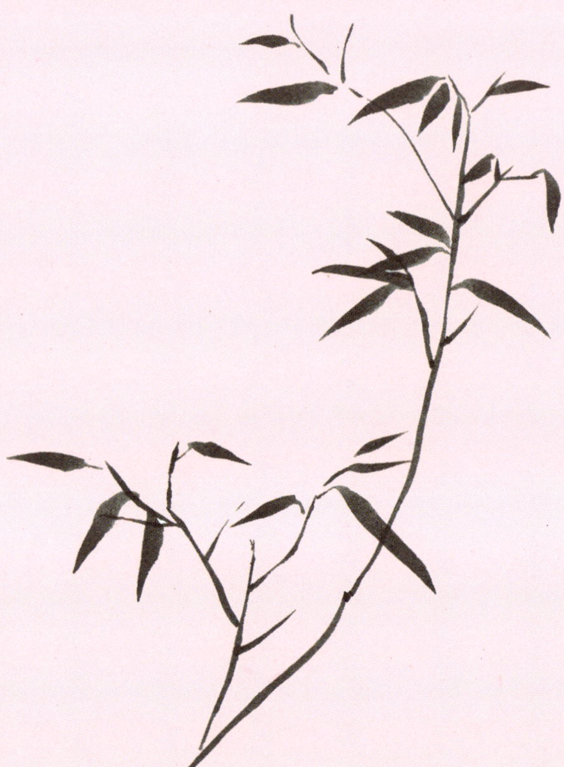

Goofy Faces

Follow the different expressions in the examples to draw in the empty cartoon faces below. Colour them.

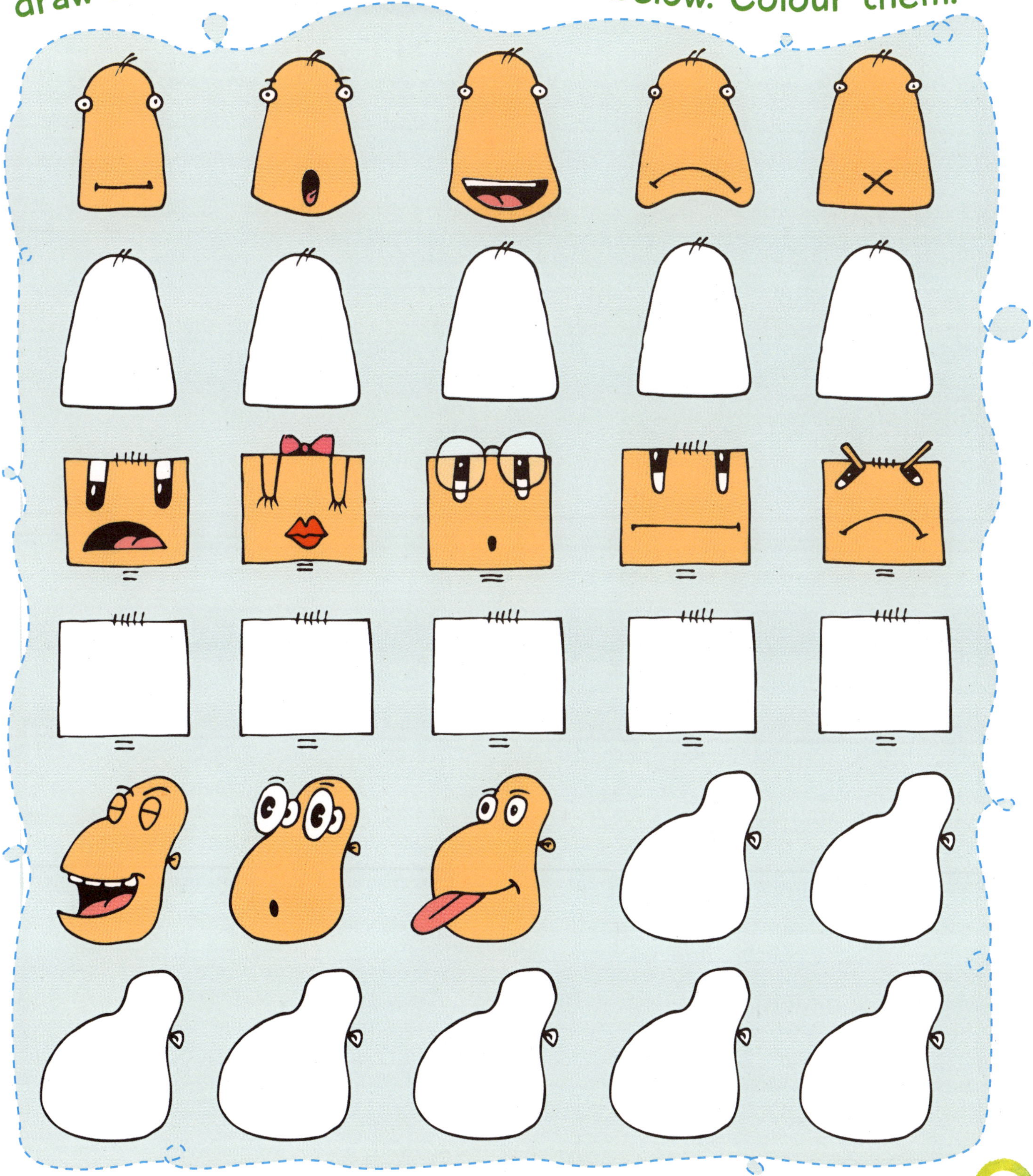

Sweet Swan

Here are six simple steps to draw a swan.

Trace over the steps before drawing one on your own.

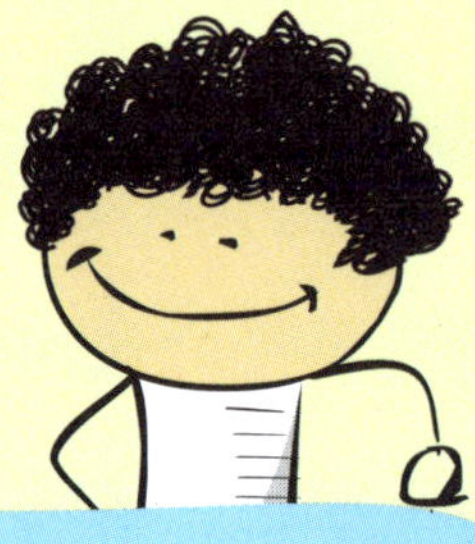

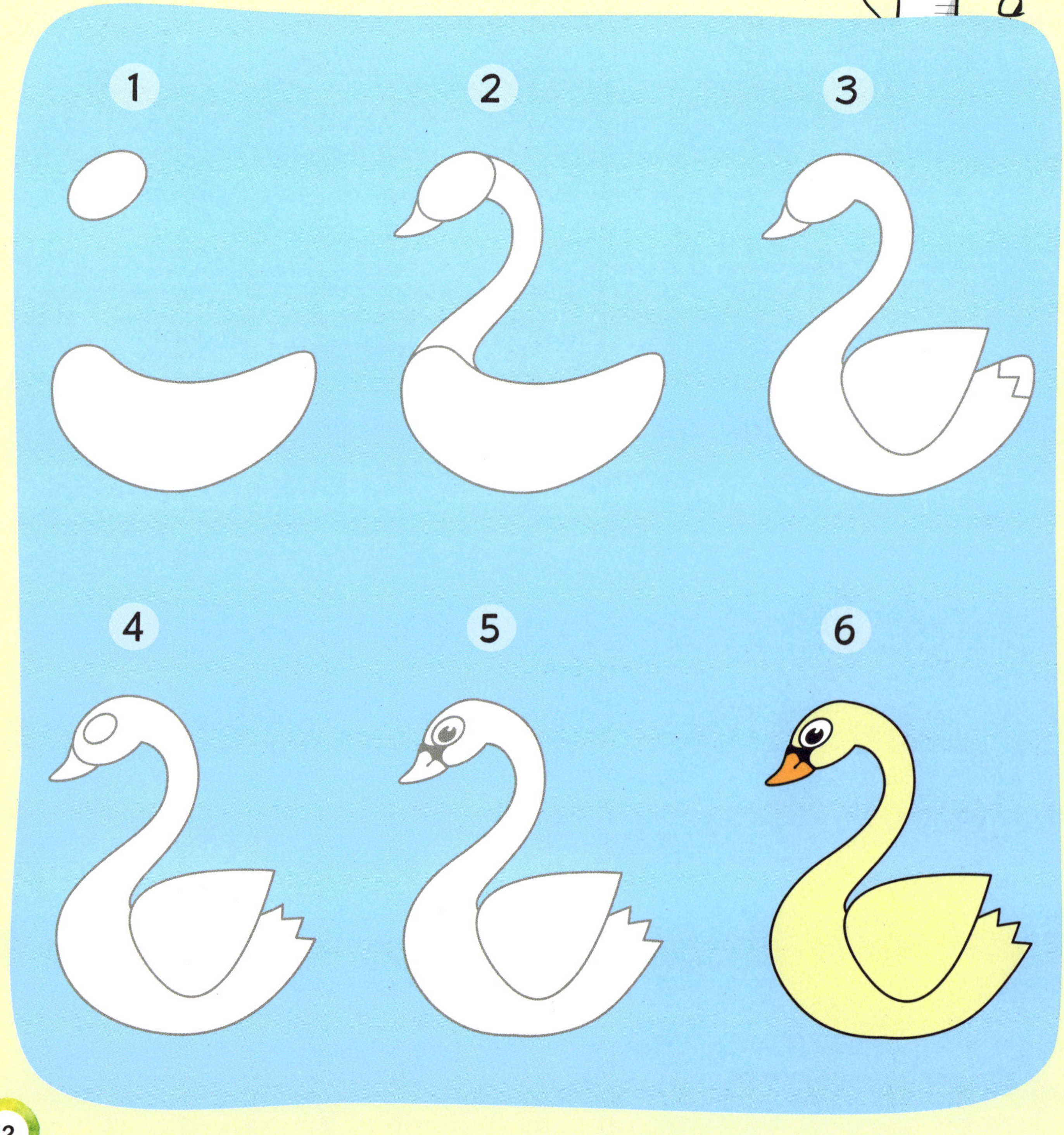

Now, draw a swan in a pond following the steps you learnt. Finish the picture by colouring it.

Leafy Greens

Did you know that when yellow and blue are mixed, we get green? First, paint the leaf below in yellow. Use a thin brush to make light blue strokes over it. The end result will be green. Try it out!

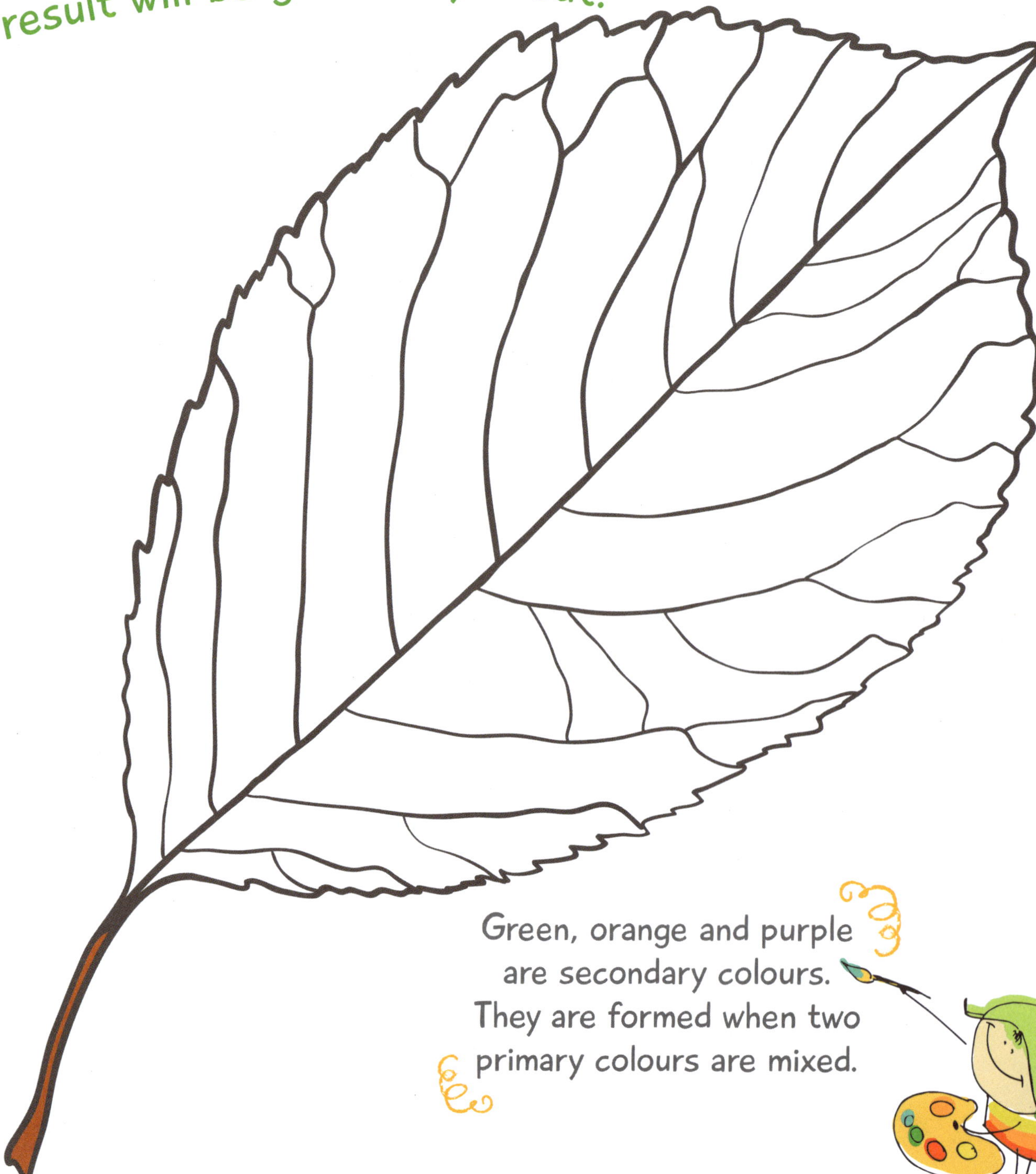

Green, orange and purple are secondary colours. They are formed when two primary colours are mixed.

Autumn Oranges

Paint the back of the leaf with red and press it in the space below. On the same leaf, add a coat of yellow paint and press it on the paper again. Doesn't it remind you of autumn? Do this multiple times to see different shades of orange.

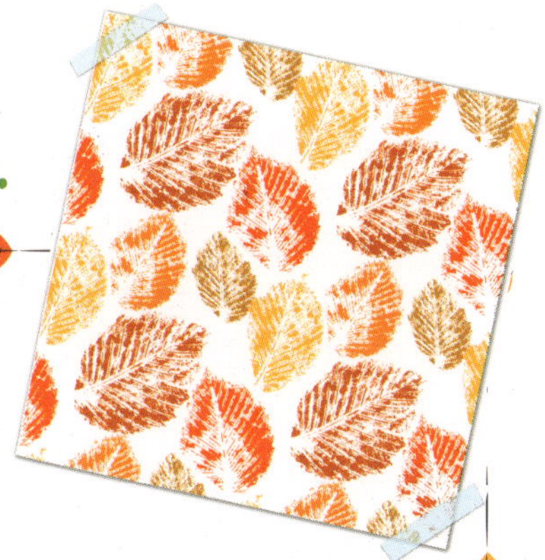

Midnight Hues

Paint the midnight sky. Dip a toothbrush in blue paint and spray it in the box below. Then, spray over it with red paint. Doesn't the purple colour look like the midnight sky?

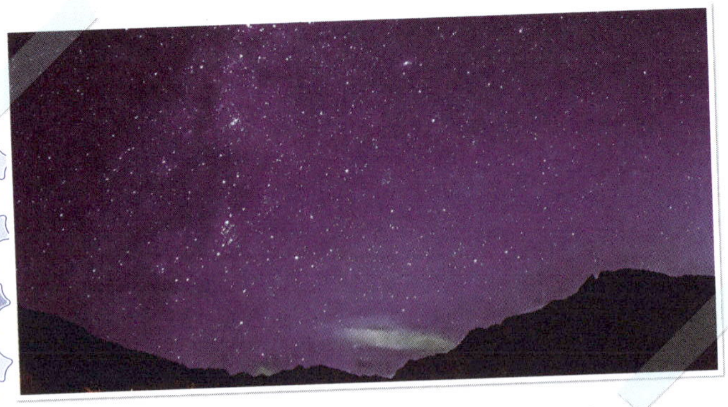

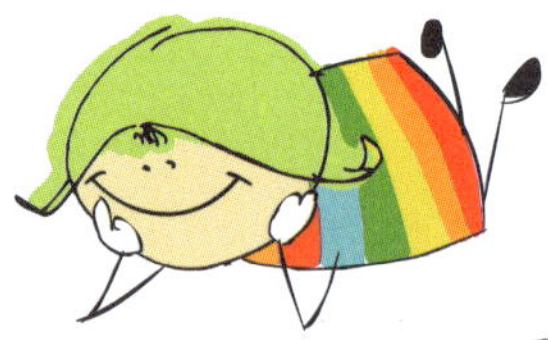

Add stars to the sky by adding white spots after the other colours have dried.

Optical Art

Trace over the shapes to complete these optical illusions. Try to copy them in the boxes alongside.

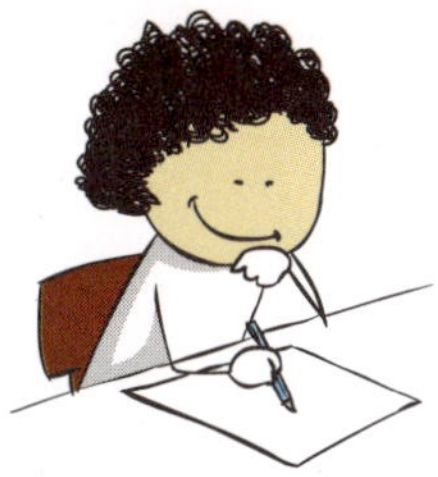

Begin by drawing three squares, one inside the other.

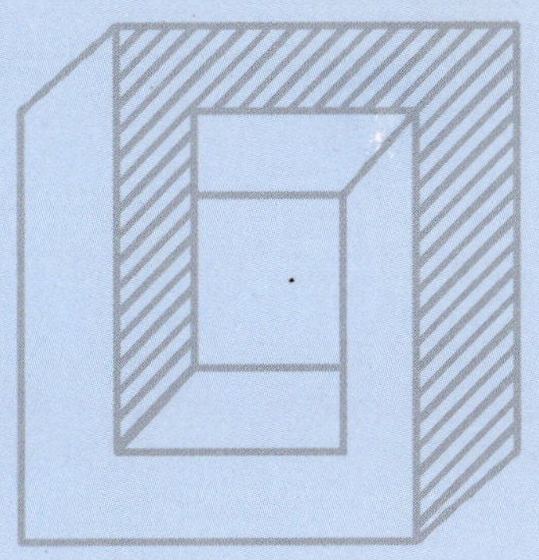

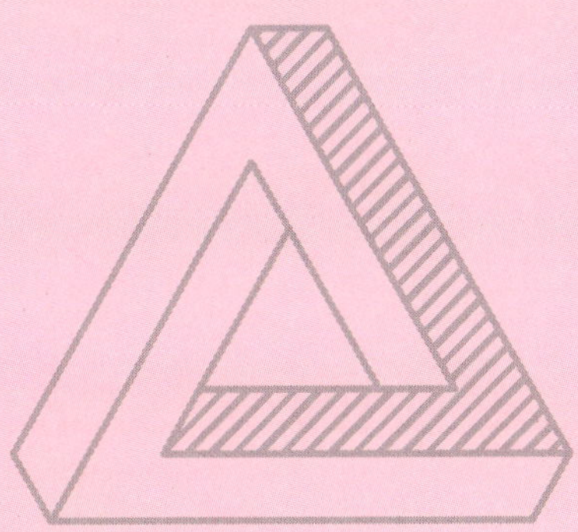

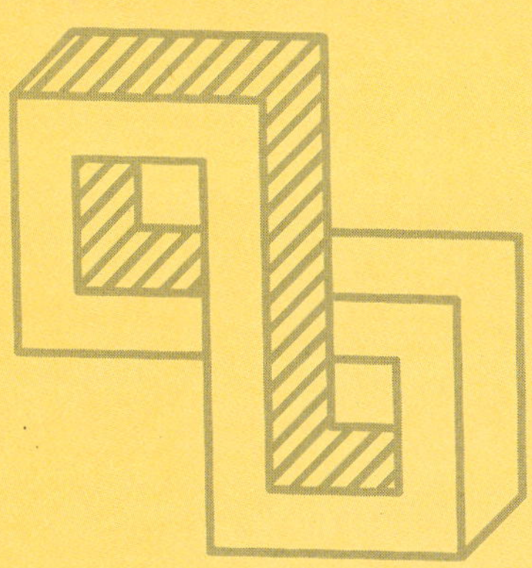

Tick Tock

Follow these five steps to draw an alarm clock.

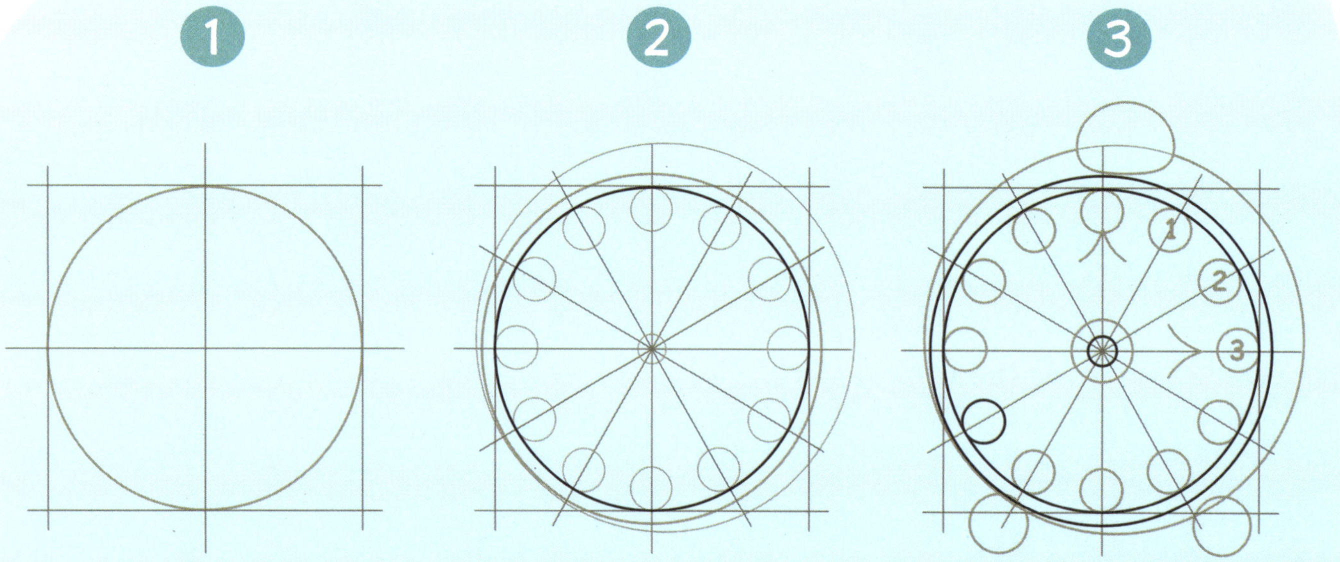

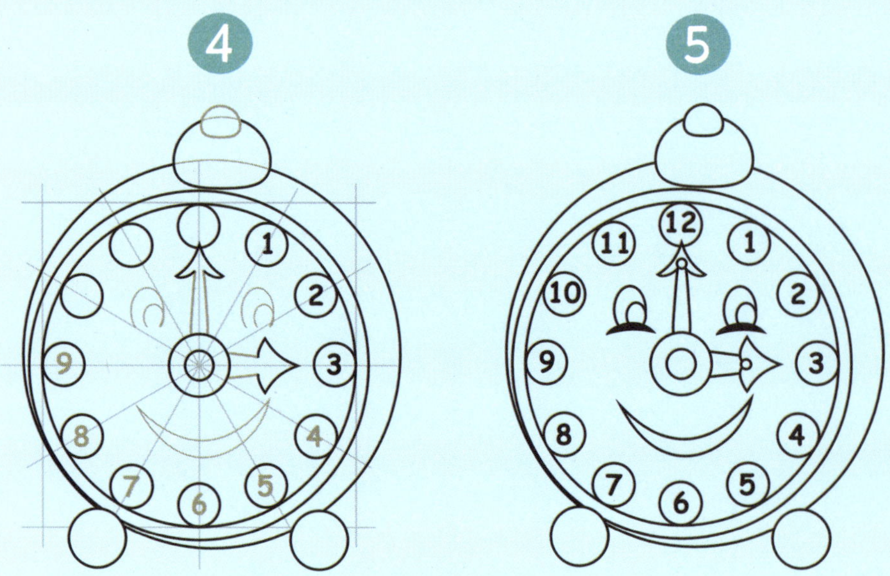

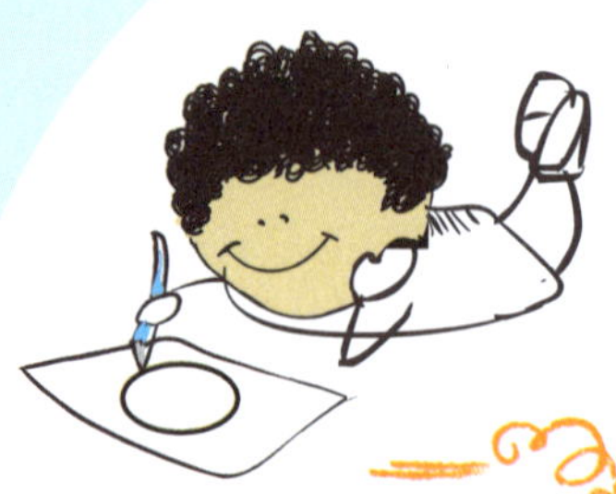

Practice each step a few times so that the end result is good.

Now, draw the alarm clock and colour it in any way you want to.

Waxed Up

Instead of a pencil, use a candle or a white wax crayon to draw a snowy scene. You can draw a snowman and snowflakes too. Paint over it with watery blue paint and watch the magic.

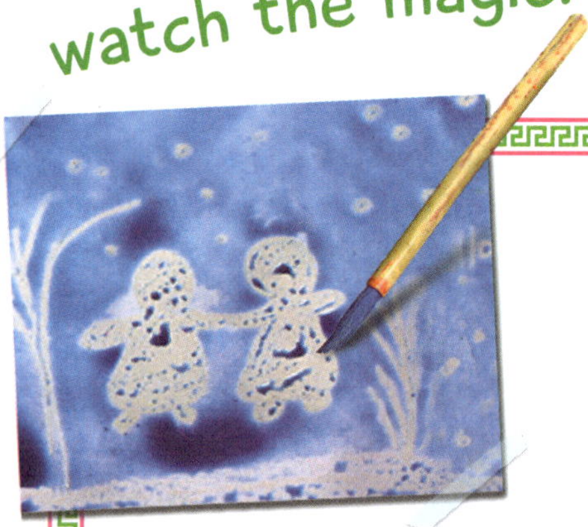

Mandala Designs

Trace over this mandala design and colour it.

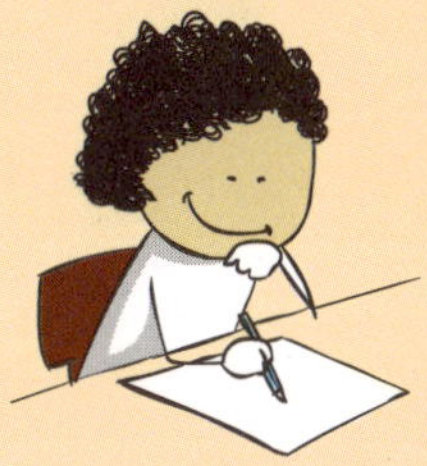

Use bright, contrasting colours for the design.

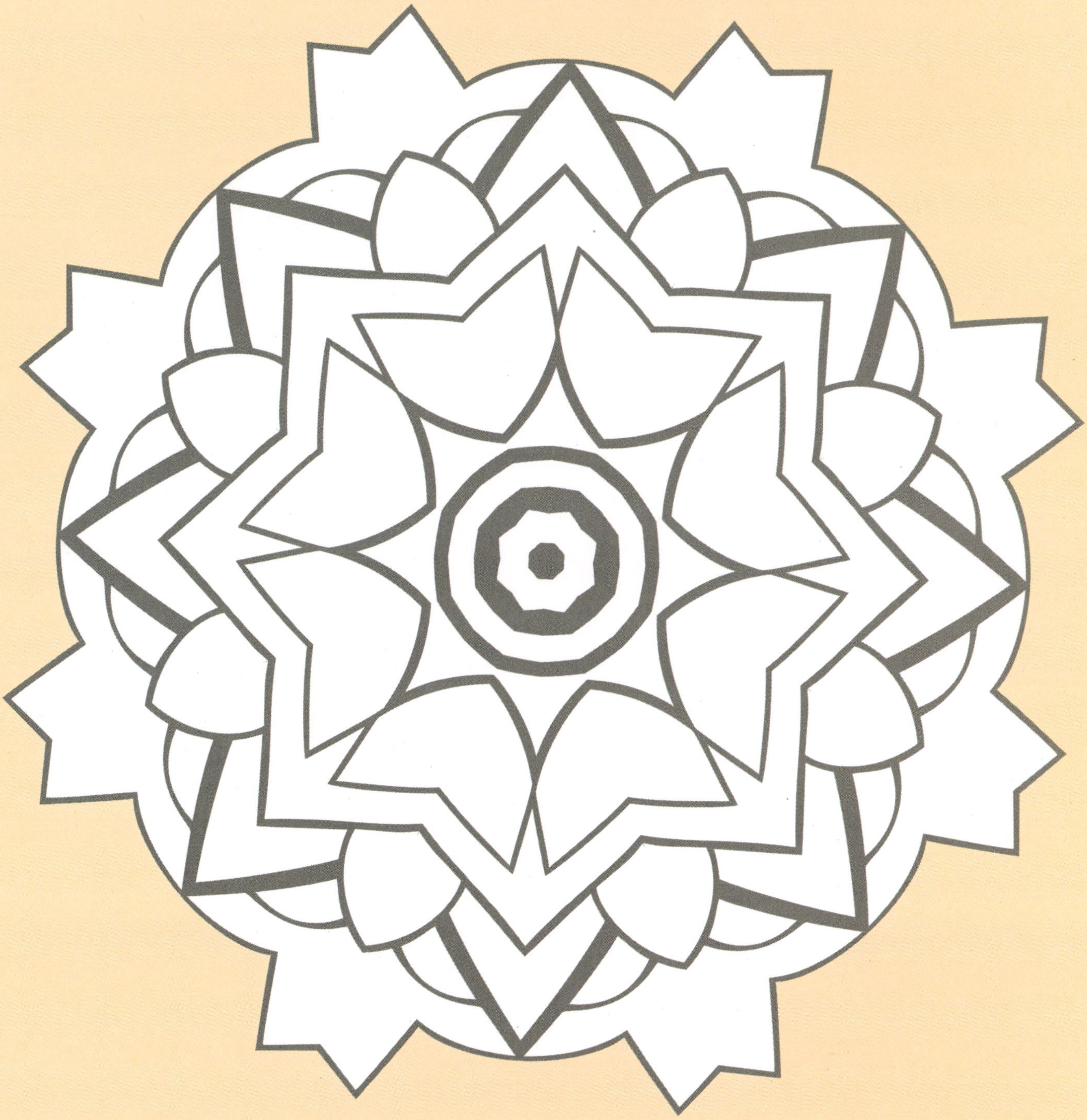

The Last Straw

Put a blob of watery paint at the bottom of the page. Use a straw to blow the paint in an upward direction. Dip the back of a pencil in green, yellow or orange paint and press it to make it look like leaves on a branch.

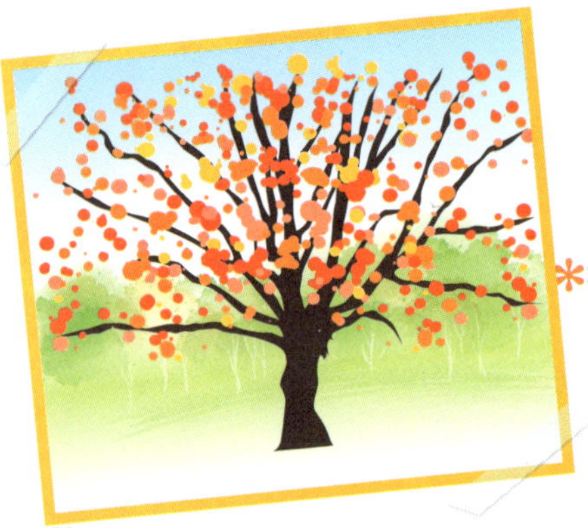

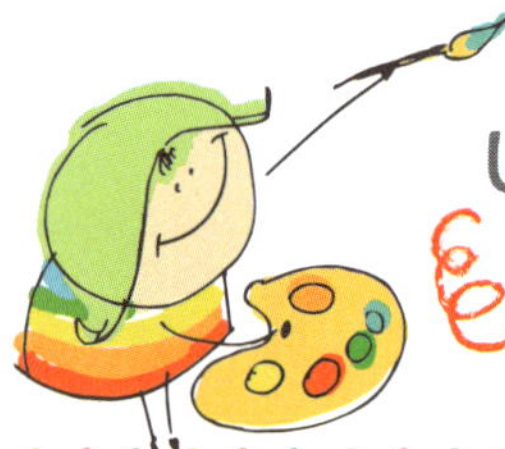

Use black crayon to give your painting solid outlines.

Patterned Fun

Complete the pattern in each box using different colours.

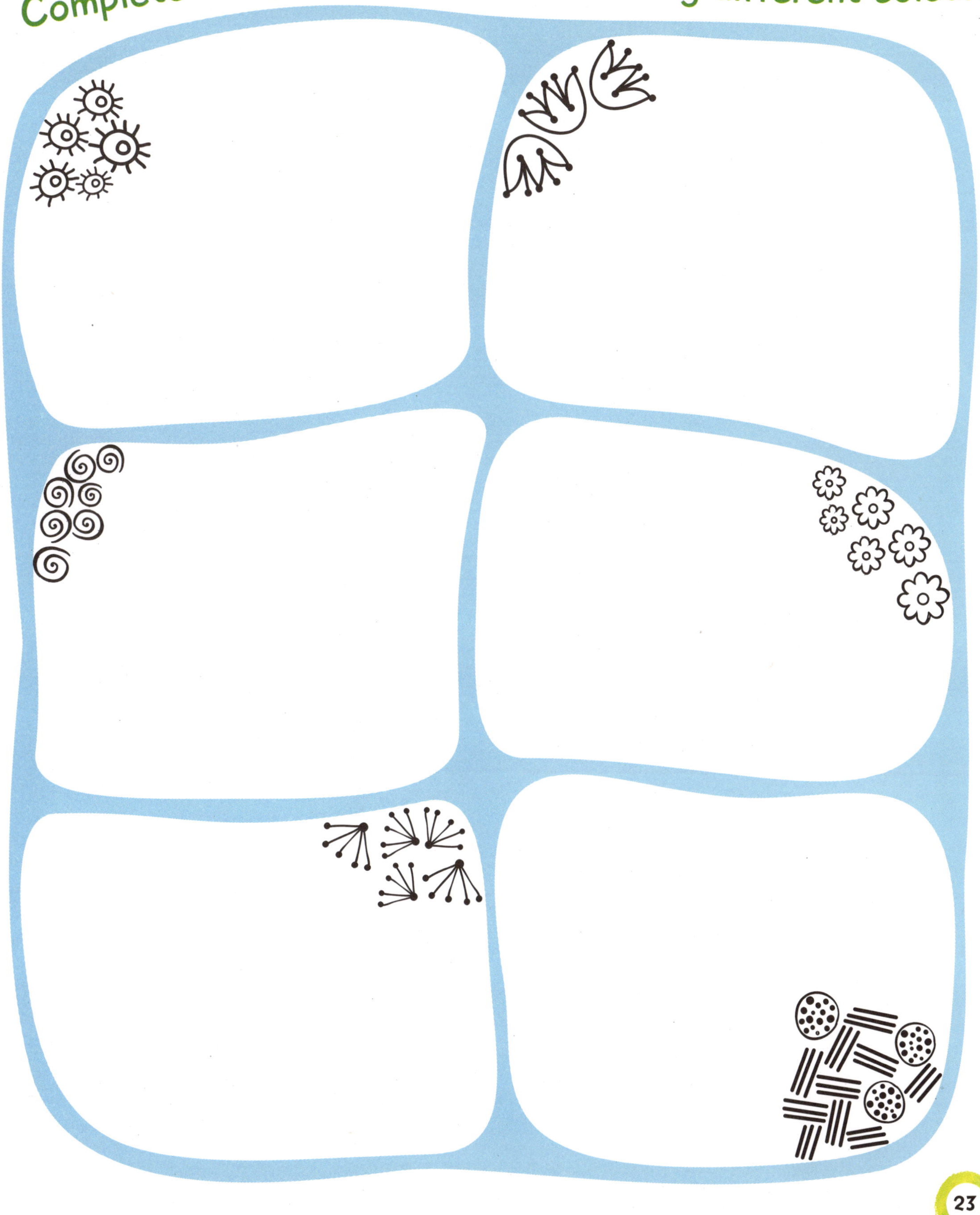

Fun with Water

Wet the paper with a flat brush. Dip another brush in paint and paint over the wet paper with it.

Keep your water colours ready as the water on the page can dry off.

Watery Scene

Wet the paper with water and use your water colours to paint a landscape.

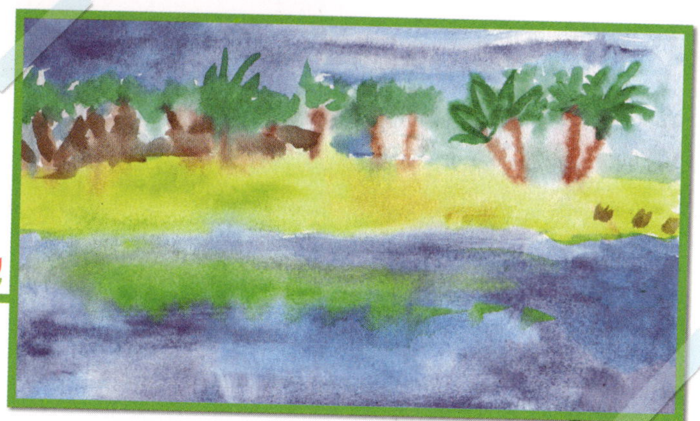

Hairy Designs

You and your best friend have different hairstyles. Give these faces different hairstyles too.

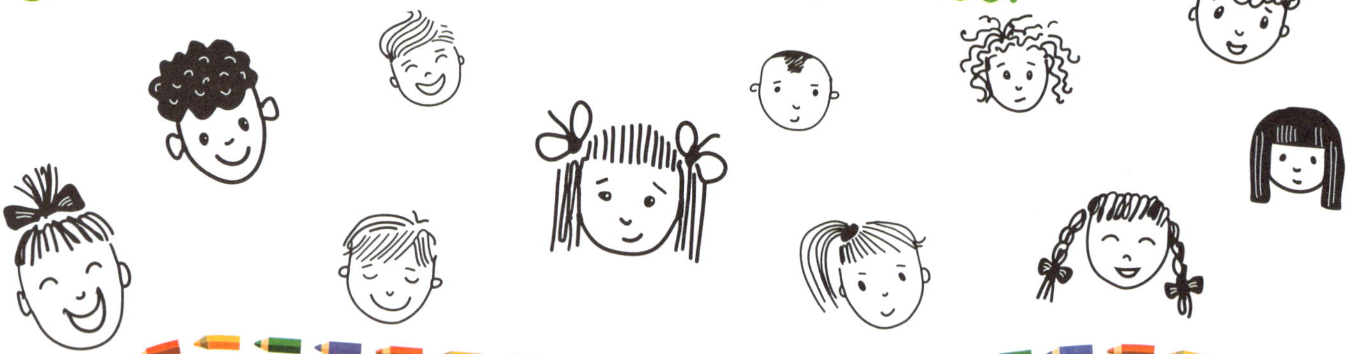

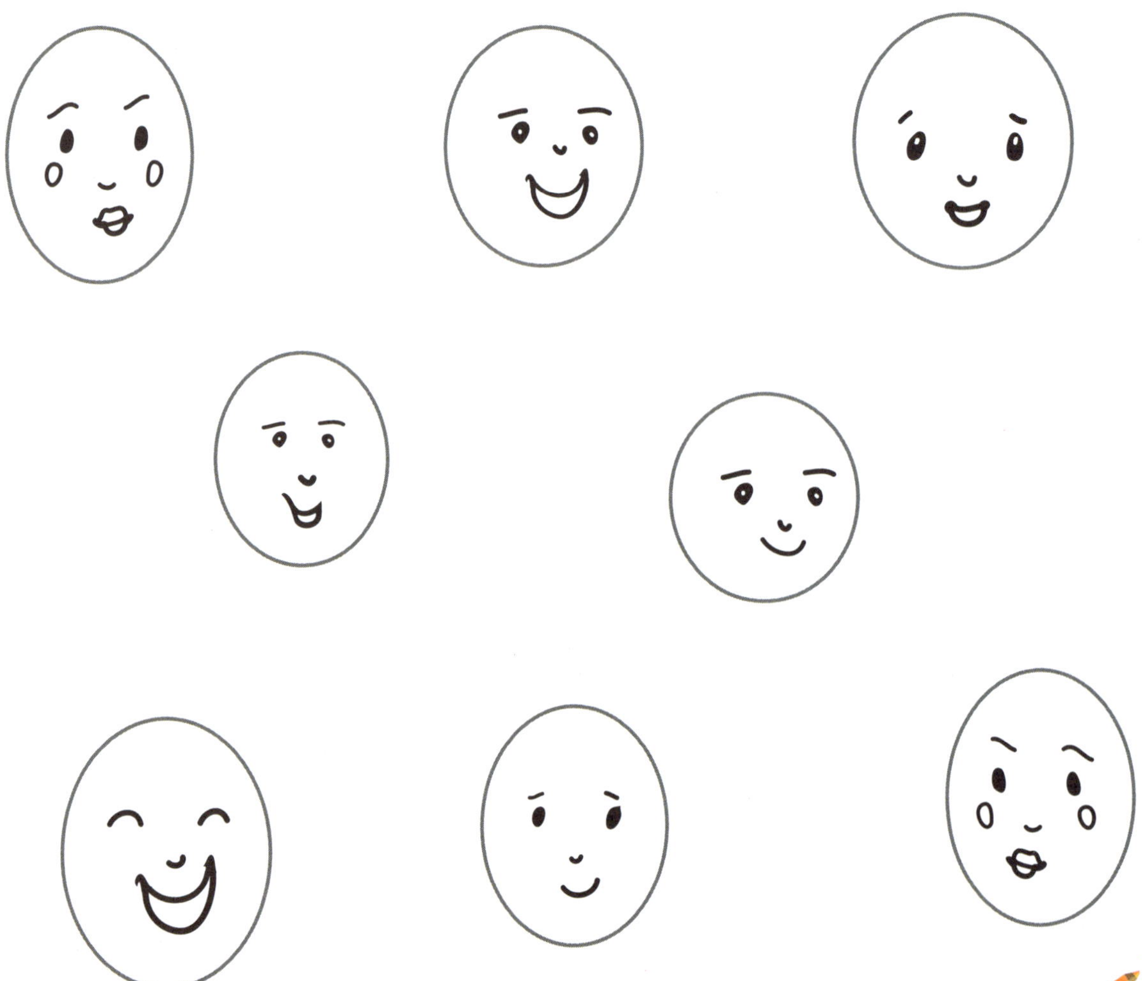

Out in the rain

Paint a scene of a child playing in the rain. She or he could be jumping in mud puddles or playing with paper boats.

Use paints to make this scene pretty and colourful.

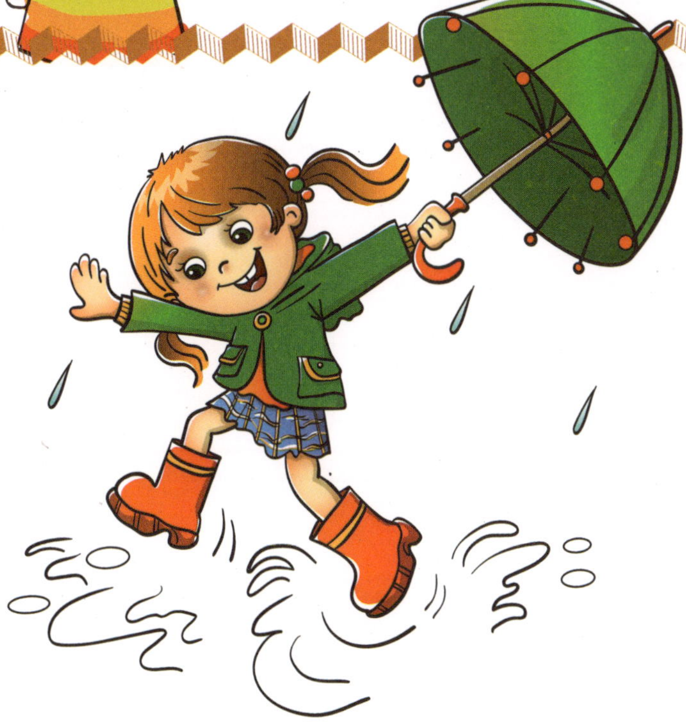

Letter Art

Use a thick sketch pen and write your favourite word in a dotted outline below. Use a sketch pen of a different colour to join the dots and complete the word.

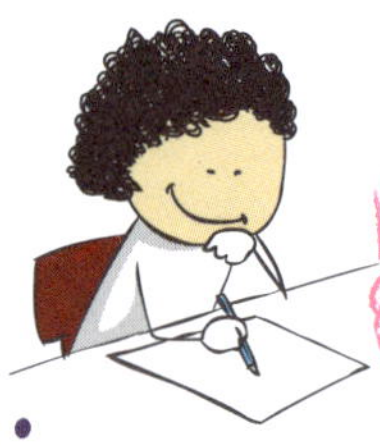

You can use glitter and other coloured sketch pens to decorate the word.

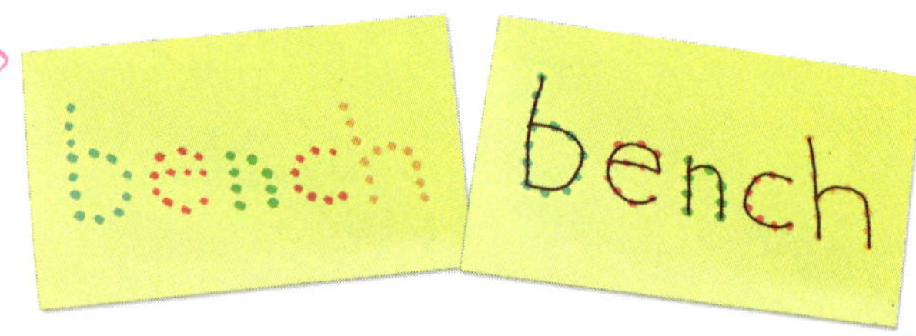

Paint on a Foil

Stick a piece of foil on the space given below. Paint different fishes and seaweed using acrylic paints over it to make an aquarium.

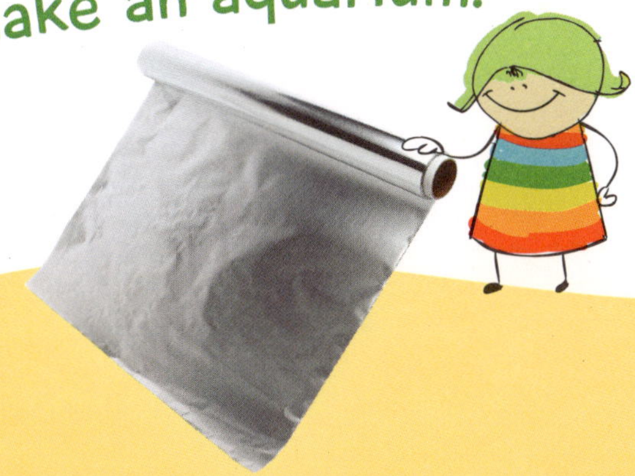

Use bright paints for the fish and blue for the water.

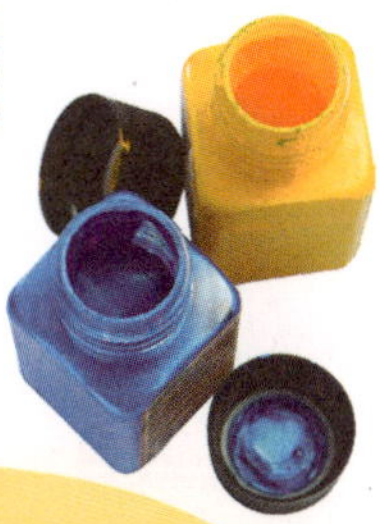

Christmas Delight

Make a Christmas Tree and decorate it using twigs as a brush. You can even cut out vegetables to make stars and baubles.

You will need:

- Potatoes and Okra (Lady Fingers)
- Paints
- Brush
- Paper
- Glitter
- Twigs

Follow these steps to make the Christmas tree:

1. Take twigs, dip it in green colour and paint the Christmas Tree.
2. Now take the vegetable shapes and decorate the tree with baubles.
3. Use the glitter to add the streamers.

Roll Puppets

Make you own roll puppets out of tissue rolls.

You will need:
- Tissue paper rolls
- Card paper
- Paints
- Black sketch pen

Follow these steps to make your puppet:

1. Paint tissue rolls with bright colours.
2. Cut out different shapes from the card paper for the eyes. Stick them on the tissue roll.
3. Use the black sketch pens to make the 6 eyebrows, nose and mouth.
4. Put your hand into the roll and make your puppet move around.

Your roll puppet is ready.

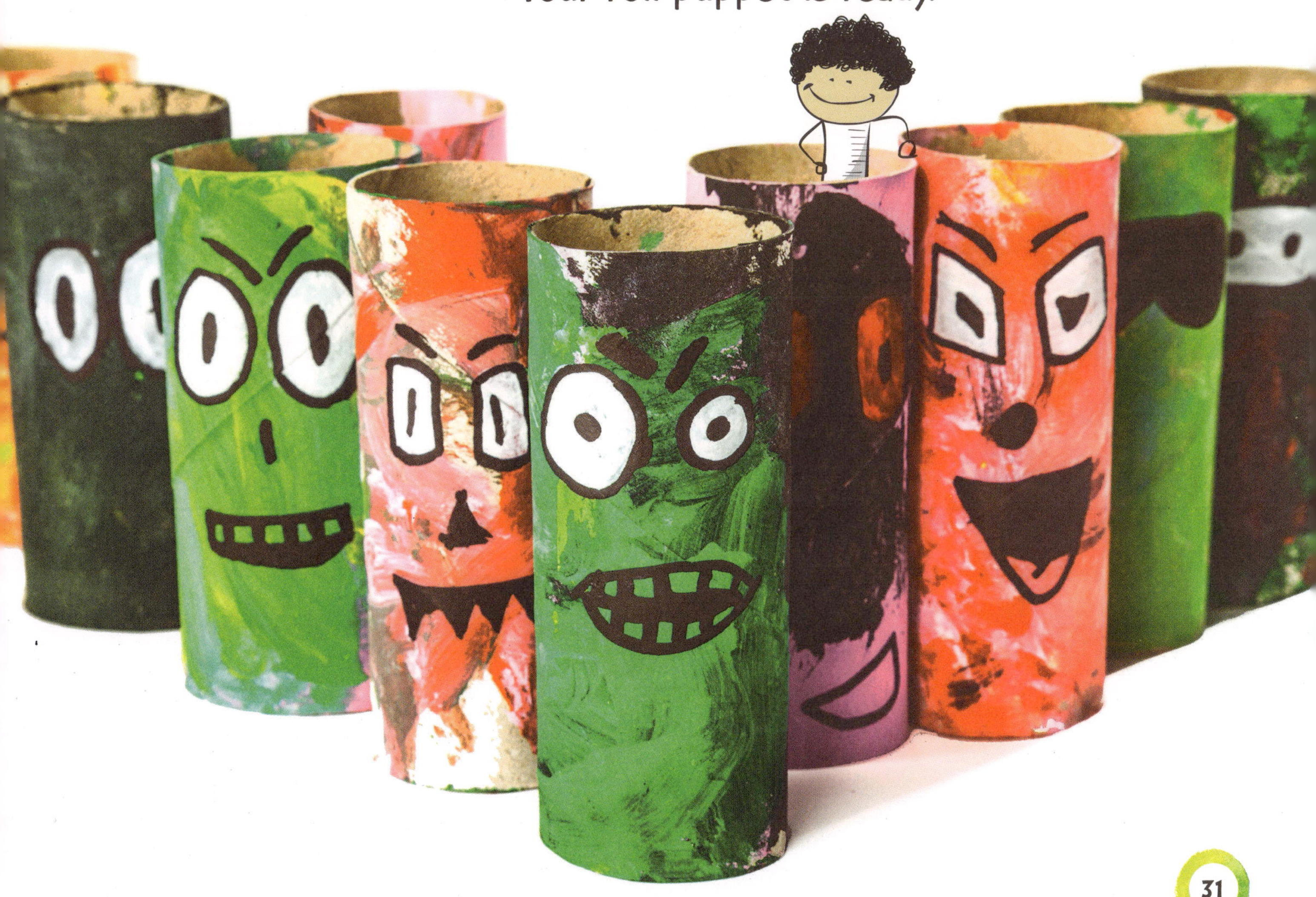

Find Me!

Follow the code to colour this picture and find the hidden picture.

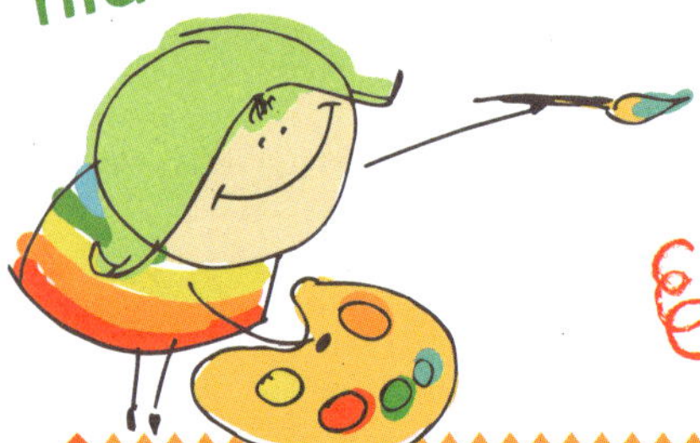

Find all the blocks with the same number and colour them. Then, move on to the next number.

1 2

3 4

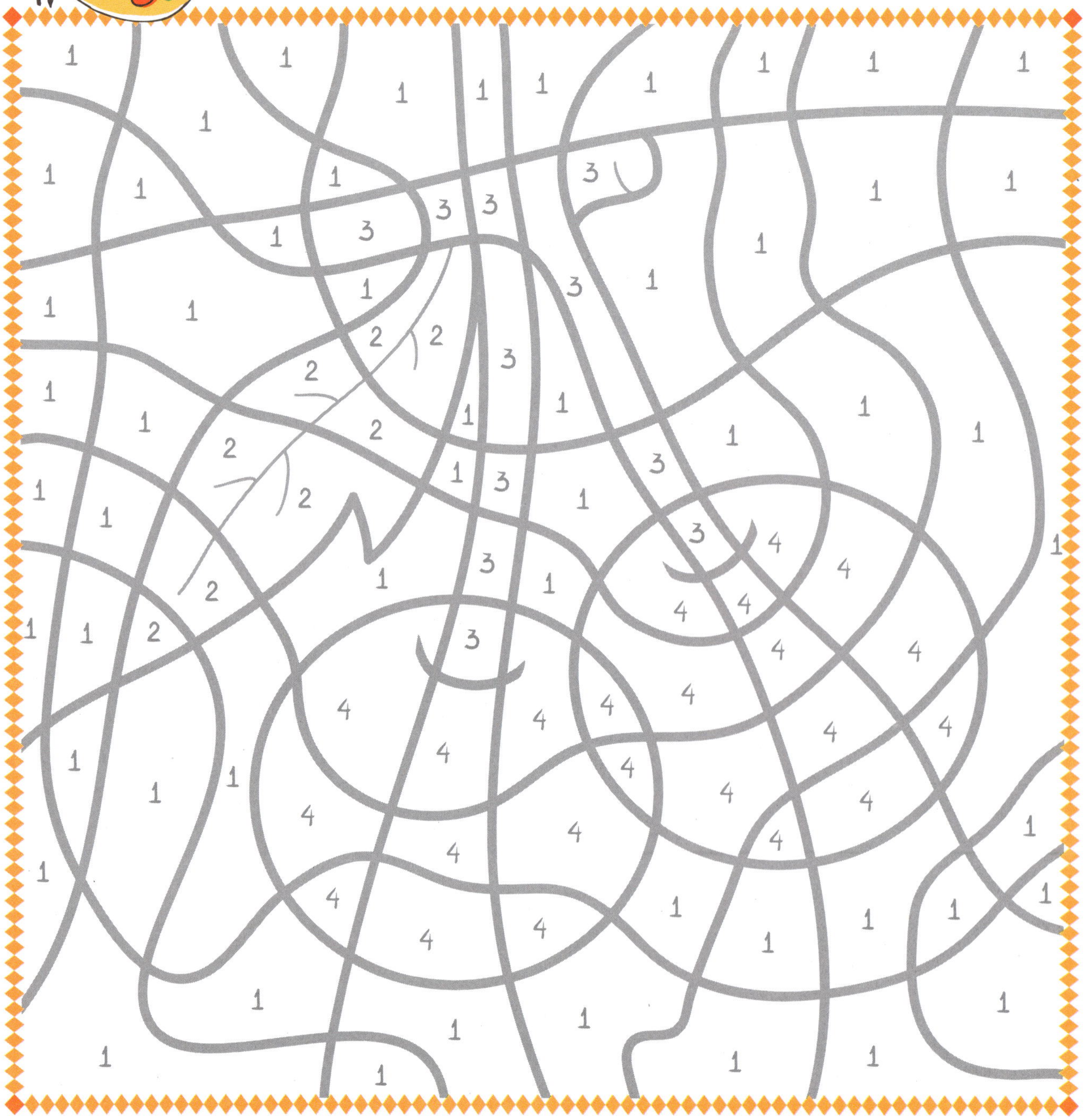